HONEST QUOTES FROM LAWYERS

SINCE THE
BEGINNING OF TIME

Intentionally left blank

Intentionally left blank

Intentionally left blank

Intentionally left blank

Intentionally left blank

Intentionally left blank

8

Intentionally left blank

Intentionally left blank

Intentionally left blank

Intentionally left blank

Intentionally left blank

Intentionally left blank

Intentionally left blank

Intentionally left blank

Intentionally left blank

Intentionally left blank

Intentionally left blank

Intentionally left blank

Intentionally left blank

Intentionally left blank

Intentionally left blank

Intentionally left blank

Intentionally left blank

Intentionally left blank

26

Intentionally left blank

Intentionally left blank

Intentionally left blank

Intentionally left blank

Intentionally left blank

Intentionally left blank

Intentionally left blank

Intentionally left blank

Intentionally left blank

Intentionally left blank

36

Intentionally left blank

Intentionally left blank

38

Intentionally left blank

Intentionally left blank

Intentionally left blank

Intentionally left blank

Intentionally left blank

Intentionally left blank

Intentionally left blank

Intentionally left blank

Intentionally left blank

Intentionally left blank

Intentionally left blank

Intentionally left blank

Intentionally left blank

Intentionally left blank

Intentionally left blank

Intentionally left blank

Intentionally left blank

Intentionally left blank

Intentionally left blank

Intentionally left blank

Intentionally left blank

Intentionally left blank

Intentionally left blank

Intentionally left blank

Intentionally left blank

Intentionally left blank

Intentionally left blank

.

Intentionally left blank

Intentionally left blank

Intentionally left blank

Intentionally left blank

Intentionally left blank

Intentionally left blank

Intentionally left blank

Intentionally left blank

Intentionally left blank

Intentionally left blank

Intentionally left blank

Intentionally left blank

Intentionally left blank

Intentionally left blank

Intentionally left blank

Intentionally left blank

Intentionally left blank

Intentionally left blank

Intentionally left blank

Intentionally left blank

Intentionally left blank

Intentionally left blank

Intentionally left blank

Intentionally left blank

Intentionally left blank

Intentionally left blank

Intentionally left blank

Intentionally left blank

Intentionally left blank

Intentionally left blank

Intentionally left blank

Intentionally left blank

Intentionally left blank

Intentionally left blank

Intentionally left blank

Intentionally left blank

Intentionally left blank

Intentionally left blank

Intentionally left blank

Intentionally left blank

Intentionally left blank

Intentionally left blank

Intentionally left blank

Intentionally left blank

Intentionally left blank

Intentionally left blank

Intentionally left blank

Intentionally left blank

Intentionally left blank

.

117

Intentionally left blank

Intentionally left blank

Intentionally left blank

Intentionally left blank

Intentionally left blank

Intentionally left blank

Intentionally left blank

Intentionally left blank

Intentionally left blank

Intentionally left blank

Intentionally left blank

129

Intentionally left blank

Intentionally left blank

Our books are both the joke and the punchline

Find More Books At:
laughoutloudbooks.com

@LOLBooks99

Facebook.com/LOLBooks99

17858341R00076

Made in the USA
Middletown, DE
11 February 2015